FIERCE FEMALES OF FICTION

STORM

X-MEN MUTANT TURNED HEROINE

KENNY ABDO

Fly!
An Imprint of Abdo Zoom
abdobooks.com

abdobooks.com

Published by Abdo Zoom, a division of ABDO, P.O. Box 398166, Minneapolis, Minnesota 55439. Copyright © 2021 by Abdo Consulting Group, Inc. International copyrights reserved in all countries. No part of this book may be reproduced in any form without written permission from the publisher. Fly!™ is a trademark and logo of Abdo Zoom.

Printed in the United States of America, North Mankato, Minnesota.
102020
012021

THIS BOOK CONTAINS
RECYCLED MATERIALS

Photo Credits: Alamy, Everett Collection, Getty Images, Shutterstock
Production Contributors: Kenny Abdo, Jennie Forsberg, Grace Hansen
Design Contributors: Dorothy Toth, Neil Klinepier, Laura Graphenteen

Library of Congress Control Number: 2020910905

Publisher's Cataloging-in-Publication Data

Names: Abdo, Kenny, author.
Title: Storm: X-Men mutant turned heroine / by Kenny Abdo
Other title: X-Men mutant turned heroine
Description: Minneapolis, Minnesota : Abdo Zoom, 2021 | Series: Fierce females of fiction | Includes online resources and index.
Identifiers: ISBN 9781098223151 (lib. bdg.) | ISBN 9781098223854 (ebook) | ISBN 9781098224202 (Read-to-Me ebook)
Subjects: LCSH: Storm (Fictitious character)--Juvenile literature. | X-Men (Fictitious characters)--Juvenile literature. | Women superheroes--Juvenile literature. | Comic strip characters --Juvenile literature. | Heroes--Juvenile literature. | Characters and characteristics in literature--Juvenile literature.
Classification: DDC 809.3--dc23

TABLE OF CONTENTS

STORM

Raining down justice and parting the dark clouds of evil, **mutant** Storm is a force of nature.

The X-Men member turned leader is considered one of the most **iconic** characters in comic book history.

BACKSTORY

Storm was created by comic book writer Len Wein and artist Dave Cockrum. Not wanting an all-male lineup for the *X-Men*, they **pitched** changing the hero Typhoon into a female.

Cockrum took the Black Cat's costume and added Jean Grey's cape. He also gave Storm stark white hair.

She debuted in the *Giant-Size X-Men* issue #1. Released in 1975, the new team included Storm, the first African-American female featured in a **mainstream** comic book.

JOURNEY

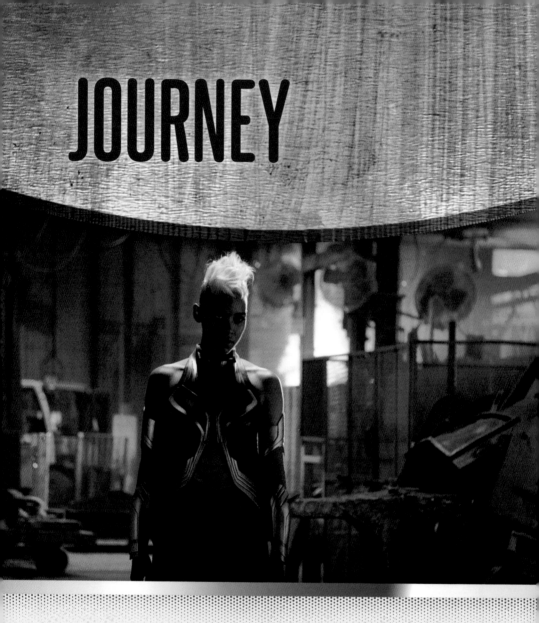

Storm was born Ororo Munroe in Harlem, New York. Her mother was the princess of a Kenyan tribe of **sorceresses**. Storm's father was an African-American photojournalist.

After her parents are tragically killed, Ororo turns to a life of crime. Then she discovers her **mutant** powers. Ororo is then recruited by Professor X to join his new team, the X-Men.

Storm has the ability to create and control the weather. She can form tornadoes and hurricanes at will. Storm is also a strong fighter and skilled pilot.

Storm has been a key member of many superhero teams. She and her then husband, Black Panther, made up half of the Fantastic Four for a time. Storm has also fought with the Avengers.

After losing her powers, Storm challenges Cyclops to a battle to see who should head the X-Men. She wins, even without her powers, taking her rightful place as leader.

EPIC-LOGUE

Storm has appeared in more than 7,500 comic book issues. She has been featured in nine movies, played most notably by Halle Berry and Alexandra Shipp.

Taking lead of the X-Men and inspiring a generation, Storm is a hero who doesn't fit under just one umbrella.

GLOSSARY

iconic – commonly known for excellence.

mainstream – a leading trend within entertainment.

mutant – an organism or person that is changed through their genes and DNA to become something different than usual.

pitch – an idea for a character by a writer or creator.

sorceress – a female who has magical powers.

ONLINE RESOURCES

Booklinks
NONFICTION NETWORK
FREE! ONLINE NONFICTION RESOURCES

To learn more about Storm, please visit **abdobooklinks.com** or scan this QR code. These links are routinely monitored and updated to provide the most current information available.

INDEX